VIRUSES

Natalie Goldstein

Published in 2004 by The Rosen Publishing Group, Inc.
29 East 21st Street, New York, NY 10010

First Edition

Library of Congress Cataloging-in-Publication Data

Goldstein, Natalie.
Viruses/Natalie Goldstein.
    p. cm.—(Germs: The library of disease-causing organisms)
Includes bibliographical references and index.
Contents: Viruses and the body—Viruses and disease—
Retroviruses—New viruses and new treatments.
ISBN 0-8239-4496-4
1. Viruses—Juvenile literature. 2. Virus diseases—Juvenile
literature. [1. Viruses. 2. Virus diseases.]
I. Title. II. Series.
QR201.V55G65 2004
616'.0194—dc21

                           2003009697

Manufactured in the United States of America

On the cover: An electron micrograph image of the polio virus, which causes poliomyelitis.

CONTENTS

1 *Viruses and the Body*

Viruses are among the simplest living things on Earth. They are tiny bits of genetic material wrapped in a protective protein coat. A single virus is no more than a millionth of an inch in length. Viruses are so small that they can infect bacteria. Viruses are the ultimate parasites. They can do absolutely nothing on their own. Viruses must invade living cells and manipulate them in order to replicate, or copy, their own genetic material. Viruses are not cells. Cells carry out their own life functions. Viruses cannot. Cells control their own reproduction and the replication of their genes. Viruses force cells to reproduce their genes for them.

Genes consist of strands of deoxyribonucleic acid, also known as DNA. When a cell divides, its DNA is replicated, and one copy goes to each daughter cell. Another genetic substance, ribonucleic acid, or RNA, is crucial in carrying out DNA's instructions for making vital cell proteins. Some viruses contain DNA, others RNA. A virus attaches itself to the surface of a host cell.

Cells are selective about which chemicals they let in and which they keep out. Special receptors on a cell's surface permit entry only of those chemicals the cell needs. A receptor is like a lock. The needed chemical is like the key that fits into and opens the lock. Viruses mimic the keys that fit the receptors on the type of cell they seek to infect. After attaching to the receptor, the virus either enters the cell or injects its genetic material into it. The virus uses the host cell's proteins and enzymes to replicate viral genes and build new viral particles. These new viruses leave the cell and spread to a new host.

Some viruses are transmitted through the air. As everyone knows, cold viruses are spread by coughing and sneezing. Other viruses spread through contaminated food or water, from mother to child in the womb or in mother's milk, from insect bites, or from contact with infected people.

The Immune System

The human body's immune system recognizes and destroys alien invaders such as viruses. As they circulate in the blood, immune system cells come into contact with other cells. Each cell displays on its surface a sample of whatever material is being produced inside it. Immune cells can distinguish between cell materials that belong in the body and substances that don't belong. When immune cells encounter viruses or viral proteins, they destroy them.

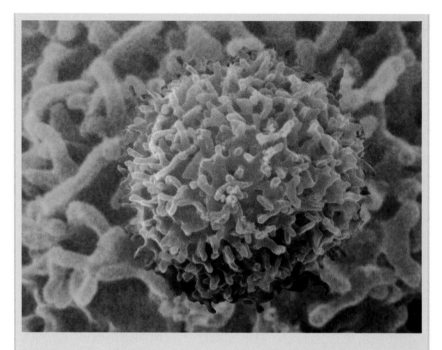

An electron micrograph of a macrophage. Macrophages are present in many major tissues and organs. They accumulate at sites of infection and engulf foreign organisms by a process called phagocytosis. They also stimulate other immune cells to respond to infection.

The immune system's first line of defense is the skin. The outer skin has layers of dead cells. Viruses infect only living cells. Unless it is cut, skin presents an impenetrable barrier to viruses. Even "inner" skin, the cells lining the mucous membranes of the mouth, nose, and eyes, can block or destroy many viruses.

If a virus does get past these barriers, the next line of defense is the leukocytes, or white blood cells, of which there are more than a dozen types. Cells such as phagocytes and macrophages work like the body's garbage collectors and consume viruses and debris from dead cells. White blood cells known as B cells also produce antibodies, chemicals that can bind to viruses and their antigens, the toxins they produce, and prevent them from entering cells. These antibodies work together with about twenty different proteins produced in the liver that can kill viruses as part of the body's complement system. If these proteins fail to kill the viruses, they bind to them. Like warning flags, they signal infection to other immune cells that can kill the viruses.

Interferon is one such "alarm protein" crucial to the complement system. Infected cells usually produce huge amounts of RNA, which triggers interferon production in the cell. As its name suggests, interferon "interferes" with viral replication in infected cells. Interferon also binds to other cells and induces them to commit suicide. Excess cell death, caused either by interferon or by viruses, activates other parts of the immune system. A full-scale attack by the

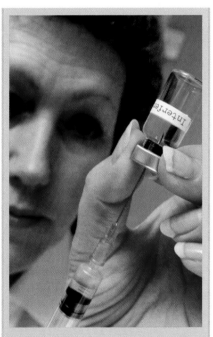

Interferon, such as that shown above being drawn into a needle, was discovered in 1957. Synthetic versions of interferon are used to treat diseases like hepatitis and multiple sclerosis.

immune system produces an inflammatory response. Inflammation results when some white blood cells release histamine, dilating blood vessels and bringing more blood and white blood cells to the site of infection.

Sometimes, a virus will invade the body and reproduce so quickly that it overwhelms the ability of antibodies and proteins to fight it. Then the body brings out its big guns—the killer T cells. T cells have surface receptors that contain random segments of proteins, so they're extremely diverse. A T cell recognizes and destroys only those viruses whose proteins match its own.

Despite this impressive armory, the immune system sometimes has trouble fighting viral infections. Many viruses can go about their business inside cells without immediately alerting the immune system. In

The Origin of Viruses

Nobody knows for sure where viruses came from. Some scientists speculate that these particles of genetic material broke away from genes in animals and plants and found a way to exist as parasites.

DNA contains "jumping genes," snippets of DNA that can detach from one part of a DNA strand and reattach at another site. Some jumping genes contain instructions for making useful proteins. It's believed that some of these gene segments found a way to leave their "home" cells and to exist parasitically as viruses.

In the early stages of life on Earth, these genes may have moved from one organism to another organism, increasing genetic diversity and aiding evolution. Now they exist independently, but they need hosts to reproduce.

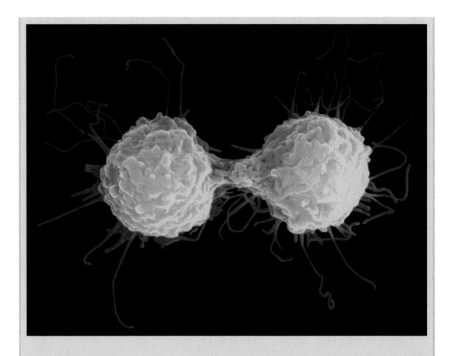

Two T-lymphocytes, a type of white blood cell that stimulates and regulates the body's immune response. When someone's T-lymphocytes are destroyed, he or she can become vulnerable to many kinds of infections.

many cases, it is not until a lot of interferon is produced by infected cells or until many cells have died that the immune system is activated. Viruses also use a variety of ingenious strategies to outwit the immune system or at least to hold it off long enough to allow them to reproduce and spread.

2 Viruses and Disease

Viruses cause many diseases, both common and serious. The common cold is caused by any one of 150 types of rhinovirus. Rhinoviruses are spread in the droplets infected people release into the air when they cough or sneeze. Rhinoviruses infect the more exposed, relatively cooler tissues of the nose, mouth, and upper airway.

Rhinoviruses contain a single strand of RNA. After binding to a cell surface, a rhinovirus injects its genetic material into the cell cytoplasm. The virus's genetic material contains one protein that causes the cell to begin copying viral RNA. The cell is forced to make numerous copies of the virus's RNA very quickly. Each new virus is then enclosed in a protein coat. The newly created viruses burst out of the cell, killing it. Within days after infection, phagocytes and natural killer cells destroy the virus, and the cold passes.

Influenza

There are three types of influenza virus—A, B, and C. Influenza A is the deadliest and also the most devious. Influenza A targets respiratory cells. The virus has a surface protein that matches receptor proteins on the respiratory cells. The protein attaches to the receptor and coats itself with some cell membrane. Then the virus enters the cell. Once inside, the virus sheds its protective coat and releases its genes—short segments of single-stranded RNA—into the cytoplasm. The RNA moves into the cell nucleus, where viral gene replication occurs.

Influenza A carries an enzyme called polymerase, which switches an infected cell from its resting mode to its reproducing mode and makes it replicate viral RNA. Polymerase is an efficient tool for replicating viral RNA, but it's not very precise. Many mistakes are made in copying the viral RNA. Genetic copying mistakes are called mutations. Influenza A's RNA replication is so prone to error that many of the replicated viruses are mutants. This is the immune

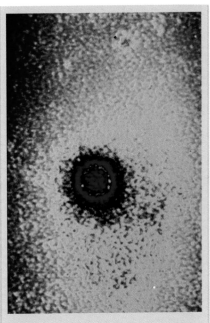

Rhinoviruses like this one are members of a group called picornaviruses. "Pico" refers to their small size, "r-n-a" to their core of RNA. This group also includes the viruses that cause polio and foot-and-mouth disease.

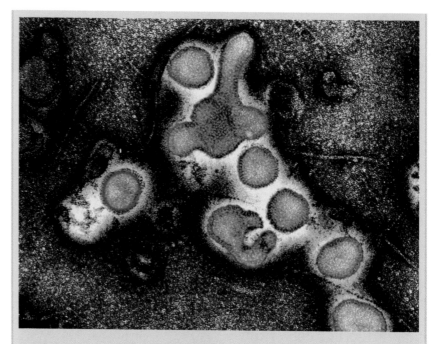

An electron micrograph of an influenza A virus magnified 62,500 times. Most influenza is not deadly, and an infected person will begin to recover in three to five days. Sometimes, however, a strain of influenza becomes deadly, weakening the host's immune system and leaving him or her susceptible to infections such as pneumonia and bronchitis.

system's worst nightmare. Influenza A is so successful because its genes are constantly changing.

Just hours after the initial infection, thousands of new viruses are created in the respiratory cells. This should trigger production of enormous quantities of interferon and activate the immune system. However, influenza A has a protein that partially disables interferon production in infected cells. This strategy buys the virus enough time to reproduce and spread. Eventually, though, the death of so many respiratory cells triggers an immune response. The infected person develops antibodies against influenza A.

However, the virus mutates so often that the immune system's defense against one strain is useless against a mutant strain. This is why the flu is longer lasting and more serious than the common cold.

Measles

The measles virus is also spread through the air. This virus can infect the whole body because it has a surface protein that can connect to receptors on most body cells. The measles virus contains a single strand of RNA. Measles's surface proteins bind to cell receptors, and the virus's RNA is injected into the cytoplasm. Measles also carries its own polymerase to get the cell to replicate viral RNA in the cytoplasm. New measles viruses bud from the infected cell and are carried in the blood to uninfected cells.

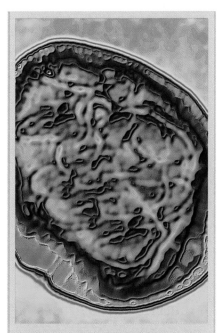

This is an electron micrograph of a measles virus. Measles mainly affects children and produces fever and a rash that often begins on the face. Because of immunizations, measles is fairly rare in developed countries.

Curiously, another reason that measles successfully infects the whole body is because it allows macrophages to kill it during its initial symptomless invasion of the lungs. As these viruses are killed, immune system cells carry samples of viral proteins to the lymph nodes. But the virus has actually infected these cells. The infected cells pass on the viral proteins to other immune cells in the lymph nodes. Infected immune cells carry the virus into the bloodstream and infect cells throughout the body. Epithelial cells are especially targeted, causing the typical measles skin rash. Only killer T cells are able to finally destroy the virus. There's only one strain of measles, and it doesn't mutate. After infection, your body produces enough antibodies to prevent reinfection, and you should have lifetime immunity.

Viruses in the Gut

Enteric adenoviruses infect the intestines. They are spread when virus-contaminated water, food, or feces is ingested. The disease is most prevalent where unsanitary conditions exist. Millions of children die every year from adenovirus-induced diarrhea.

Enteric adenoviruses have a stronger protein coating that enables them to withstand acids in the digestive tract as they head toward the intestines. Eventually, these acids eat partway through the coating, and the virus's genetic material is free to infect cells. An adenovirus's double-stranded DNA is injected into a cell's nucleus. Viral proteins trigger viral DNA replication. In two days, one infected cell can produce 100,000 adenoviruses.

The slow but sure strategy of adenovirus replication might make it vulnerable to immune attack. But the virus is prepared and armed. The adenovirus contains proteins that prevent the death of infected and neighboring cells, thus cell death does not trigger the immune system. Also, adenovirus proteins prevent the infected cell from displaying viral material on its surface, so killer T cells are not alerted to the infection. Another viral protein prevents attack by natural killer cells. Only after the virus has spread throughout the intestines are these immune cells finally able to combat it.

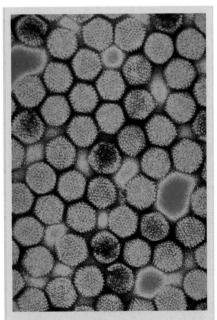

In humans, adenoviruses may cause viral gastroenteritis and infections of the upper respiratory tract, eyes, and lymph nodes. Adenoviruses can also cause several diseases in dogs, birds, mice, cattle, pigs, and monkeys.

Hepatitis

The hepatitis A virus is also spread by contaminated food, water, and waste. Like the adenovirus, it enters the body through the mouth. However, hepatitis A targets liver cells. There is only one strain of hepatitis A. The well-armored, acid-resistant virus enters the mouth and makes its way through the digestive tract to the intestines. Here, the virus infects cells and reproduces much like a rhinovirus—with one important difference. Cold viruses usually kill infected cells. Hepatitis A is a kinder, gentler virus and rarely kills infected cells.

In the intestines, hepatitis A produces a limited infection that is easily mopped up by the immune system's B cells. But the B cells carry it from the intestines to the liver for disposal, so what was a weak intestinal virus becomes a powerful disease agent. Infected liver cells make countless copies of hepatitis A's single-stranded RNA before an immune response in the liver finally finishes them

Coevolution of Viruses and their Hosts

As a virus mutates to evade the immune system, immune cells also mutate to combat the virus. Over time, a species continually infected with a particular virus evolves a natural resistance to it. The virus, too, finds ways to exploit "chinks" in the immune system armor that allow it to persevere. Over millions of years of coevolution (evolving together), viruses and their hosts reach a kind of balance, though viruses often have the edge, as they mutate much more rapidly.

Coevolution also enables viruses to find and adapt to new hosts. Herpes viruses, for example, have evolved to infect an incredible variety of hosts— even oysters. It's likely that an ancient ancestor—a single herpes virus—infected and then adapted to each new host it found.

off. Meanwhile, the new viruses move from the liver to the bile ducts, back into the intestines, then out of the body with feces. The virus spreads so effectively because it lasts a long time outside the body, remaining viable for weeks in dried feces.

Hepatitis B also infects liver cells. Its double-stranded DNA is replicated in the infected cell's nucleus. Its replication strategy is truly bizarre, involving production of RNA, which makes a "backward" copy of DNA, which is then used to make "right-side-up" copies of DNA. While all this complicated copying is going on, viral coatings are being constructed out of cell proteins. Some coatings form around and enclose a copy of the virus's DNA. Other coatings form around nothing! In fact, about 1,000 empty "decoy" viral envelopes exit the cell for every DNA-filled envelope. When B cells are finally activated, they are so busy binding to empty virus envelopes that

An image of hepatitis B, which is a major health problem in developing countries. There are vaccines to prevent hepatitis B, but no effective cure has yet been found.

lots of DNA-filled envelopes escape. And because hepatitis B doesn't kill infected cells, neither cell death nor interferon production alerts other parts of the immune system.

Hepatitis B is mostly passed from mother to child in the womb or in milk. It can also be spread by direct blood-to-blood contact. Hepatitis B can cause either acute or chronic infection. An acute infection is eventually eradicated when killer T cells destroy infected liver cells. Though the viral infection is gone, lifelong liver damage may result. About 90 percent of infants born with the virus live with a chronic, symptomless hepatitis B infection. Infected females will pass hepatitis B on to their children.

Hepatitis C always causes a chronic, long-term infection. It, too, attacks and damages the liver. Hepatitis C was first identified in 1989, so not much is known about it. Yet it infects about 170 million people worldwide. It's transmitted from mother to child or through blood-to-blood contact. Hepatitis C binds to macrophages. It also attaches to lipoproteins (fat-protein complexes) in the blood. Since every body cell needs lipoproteins, all cells have receptors for it. Yet the virus "prefers" to bind to liver cells. Infected liver cells produce up to 1 trillion viruses daily!

The error rate in copying hepatitis C's genes is very large. Its constant mutations drive the immune system crazy. After the initial infection, antibodies and

The 1918 Flu Pandemic

An epidemic is a locally intense outbreak of infection. A pandemic is a worldwide outbreak. In 1918, a pandemic of influenza A infected half the world's population. Twenty million people died, with most deaths among teenagers and young adults.

Every winter produces some influenza A outbreaks. Each time, influenza A produces two or three minor mutations in its genes. Accumulation of small mutations is called antigenic drift, in which the virus slowly "drifts away" from its original genetic makeup. Antigenic shift, on the other hand, is a sudden and dramatic alteration of viral genes. This mutation has a devastating effect on host populations. Influenza A pandemics occur when antigenic shift gives rise to a new and highly virulent form of the virus.

In 1918, those killed outright by the flu virus died within two days of infection. Most others died within one or two weeks, not from the virus but from bacterial infections, especially pneumonia, that overcame the victims' weakened immune systems.

Nurses in Lawrence, Massachusetts, care for patients in outdoor tents during the 1918 influenza pandemic. It was believed that fresh outdoor air would help the patients recover.

Influenza A pandemics occur every ten to forty years. The last occurred in 1968. It's not known what triggers an antigenic shift in influenza A.

killer T cells recognize and conquer the virus. Just when the enemy seems to be wiped out, one or more mutant strains of the hepatitis C virus emerge and attack. The immune system must start from scratch to fight the mutant. This cat-and-mouse game occurs in six-week cycles. The virus is careful not to mutate too rapidly, for then it would likely kill its host. Nor does it mutate too slowly and risk being demolished by the immune system. Slow and steady mutation maintains an active and chronic infection.

Hepatitis C is spread from mother to child, mostly during childbirth. Intravenous drug users who share needles may transmit the infection in blood. Transfusion with infected blood may also spread the disease. In most cases, people with chronic hepatitis C infections suffer no symptoms for decades. Eventually, continuous cycles of infection cause cirrhosis of the liver, which can be fatal.

Human Papillomavirus

The human papillomavirus (HPV) produces skin warts. Each of the hundred or so HPVs specializes in infecting basal cells (in the innermost part of the skin) in a particular part of the body. Each has protein receptors to match those on the target basal cells. The virus's double-stranded DNA is replicated in the infected cell's nucleus. At some stage, HPV replicates wildly in basal cells, eventually pushing masses of infected cells to the skin surface, producing a wart. Physical contact spreads the virus to a new host.

Basal cells are always reproducing because skin cells must constantly be replaced. So setting up shop in basal cells is a good strategy for a virus that produces a chronic infection. HPV's tactics overcome the immune system, too. The virus produces proteins that inhibit nearby cells from committing suicide. It doesn't kill the cells it infects, so cell death doesn't trigger an immune response. HPV also doesn't produce double-stranded RNA during replication, so infected cells don't produce interferon. These strategies ensure that once you're infected with HPV, you're stuck with it. Killer T cells may destroy some HPV, but often there are "sleeper" viruses tucked away in basal cells ready to unleash another infection.

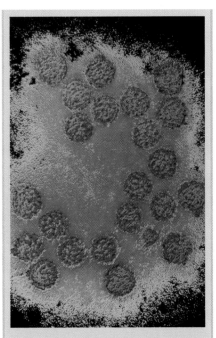

This is one of over fifty-five distinct types of human papillomavirus. Each type can cause warts or tumors on different parts of the body.

Herpes

There are several types of herpes viruses. All produce lifelong, chronic infection. Herpes viruses

Latent and Reactivating Viruses

Persistent viruses are believed to be very ancient and to have spread to humans from non-human hosts. To be persistent, viruses need a latent (hidden and inactive) period and so must take up residence in long-lived cells. Nerve cells are perfect, for they generally don't die or even age.

Reactivation of latent viruses is not fully understood. Studies have shown that stress to the body may trigger latent viruses, like herpes, to wake up, replicate, and cause an active infection. Among the factors that trigger latent herpes reactivation are psychological or physical stress, sex, fevers and colds, or exposure to ultraviolet light. These factors sometimes compromise or weaken the immune system. It's possible that persistent viruses are "aware" of the state of the immune system in an infected host. When they "sense" a weakness, viruses leave nerve cells for target cells, where they replicate and cause a new round of infection.

are transmitted by physical contact and are often transmitted sexually. Herpes simplex virus (HSV) produces a chronic infection by keeping a low profile in the body after initial infection. HSV invades epithelial cells around the skin and mucous membranes. After binding to a cell receptor, the virus fuses with the cell membrane. The virus's double-stranded DNA is injected into the cell and heads for the nucleus, where it's copied. HSV uses its proteins to take over all cellular processes. This allows the virus to replicate unhindered, killing infected cells. HSV's proteins are also employed in immune system evasion. Some HSV proteins bind with antibodies, rendering them useless. Even killer T cells are thwarted by HSV proteins. By the time the epithelial infection is defeated, the virus has

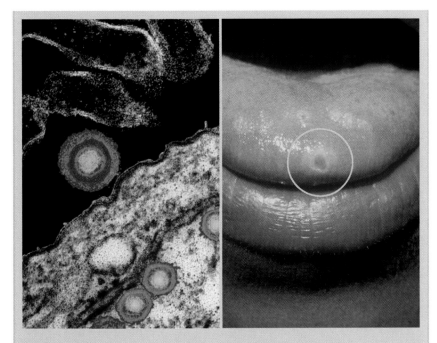

At left, an electron micrograph of a herpes simplex virus. At right, a cold sore on the tongue caused by herpes simplex 1. As many as 50 to 80 percent of adults in the United States have herpes simplex 1, which can be transmitted by kissing. They may have occasional cold sores or show no symptoms at all.

created an escape route: a cold sore. Cold sores contain thousands of viruses, ready to spread to new hosts through direct contact or through saliva.

Infection of epithelial cells is only half the HSV story. A virus spread through physical contact must remain in the body to be transmitted to others. So after leaving the epithelial cells, some HSV migrate to nearby sensory nerve cells. HSV cannot reproduce in nerve cells, but it can hide in them. Once HSV is inside nerve cells, the immune system is unaware of it. This hidden infection lasts a lifetime. Occasionally, some HSVs awake, leave the nerve

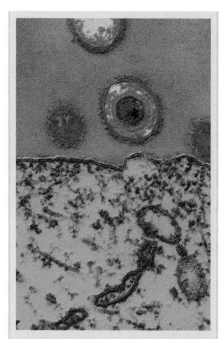

Chicken pox is a very contagious and common viral infection. Chicken pox infections occur year-round, but most occur during the winter and spring months. Most people are first exposed to chicken pox during early childhood.

cells, and reinfect epithelial cells, causing a painful skin disease.

Chicken pox is a common childhood disease caused by the herpes varicella zoster virus (VZV). The first time you get VZV, it always causes chicken pox. Chicken pox is spread by contact with its virus-filled skin blisters. B cells destroy chicken pox and produce antibodies to ensure that you never get it again. However, like HSV, VZV hides in nerve cells. VZV may remain dormant in nerve cells for decades or, if you're lucky, forever. But sometimes, VZV reawakens. When it does, it always shows up as shingles, a painful skin disorder. Shingles blisters are chock-full of VZV, and contact with them spreads the virus.

3 *Retroviruses*

Whereas many viruses carry their genetic material in the form of DNA, a retrovirus carries its genetic material as RNA. Retroviruses are unusual in that they violate what was thought to be a fundamental law of biology, that DNA forms RNA and not the other way around. But retroviral RNA is capable of working "backward" and creating viral DNA, which then creates more viral RNA to build more viruses inside the host cell.

Retroviruses generally produce no fancy proteins to control cell reproduction or to "outsmart" the immune system. They don't have to. When a retrovirus's DNA is safely tucked away inside the cell, the virus is home free. It attracts no attention from the immune system. The cell's normal reproduction ensures the persistence of the retrovirus.

HTLV1 (human T cell lymphotropic virus, type 1) was the first retrovirus discovered, in 1980. HTLV1 attaches to and infects helper T cells via an unknown receptor on the cell surface. It replicates in helper T cells. After its DNA is produced, a viral enzyme called integrase cuts the cell's DNA and inserts the viral DNA into the cell's genes. Every time the infected helper T cell reproduces, its daughter cells and all their descendants contain the virus's genes. Replication of HTLV1 is thus rather slow, depending as it does on cell division. HTLV1 doesn't kill the infected cells it relies on to reproduce it. Most of the time, HTLV1 lays low. Infected people carry it for life, but about 95 percent never suffer from an HTLV1-induced disease.

Decades after infection, about 5 percent of infected people will develop cancer. HTLV1 is associated with adult T cell leukemia. Causing a disease that kills its host (along with the virus) is an unintended result of infection. Scientists believe that leukemia arises because the viral DNA eventually causes mutations in the helper T cell's own genes. HTLV1 is spread through blood, so intravenous drug users may transmit it. It can also be spread through semen during sex. Women with HTLV1 in their blood may pass it to infants through breast milk.

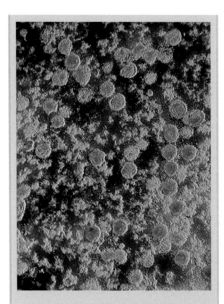

Leukemia is a cancer that causes a large increase in the numbers of white blood cells (leukocytes) in the blood or bone marrow. Cancerous T cells, like the ones above, do not fight off infection, and they also crowd out the red blood cells, making it harder for the body to use oxygen.

HIV

Another retrovirus, HIV (human immunodeficiency virus), was first identified in 1983. One year later, it was shown to cause AIDS (acquired immunodeficiency syndrome), a devastating and deadly condition that destroys the immune system.

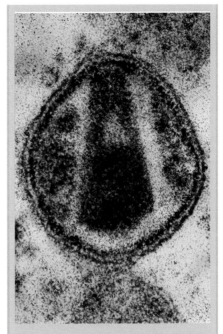

An electron micrograph of a section of an HIV virus, budding off of the membrane of a T cell. After it leaves the cell, it will enter the bloodstream and seek more cells to infect.

HIV infects immune system cells with certain surface receptors. Its primary targets are helper T cells and macrophages. HIV's RNA enters the host cell's genes in typical retrovirus fashion. However, HIV also has a protein that boosts HIV's infection rate. When an infected cell begins proliferating, this protein induces the cell to produce a thousand times more HIV genes than cell genes. The new viruses, many of them mutants, bud from the cell, enter the blood, and seek more cells to infect.

Initially, HIV infects macrophages and other cells, but it doesn't kill them. At this early stage, there are enough helper T cells to activate killer T cells, which control the HIV infection. Initial infection usually causes flulike symptoms, which disappear in a few weeks. Then HIV begins its seven- to ten-year-long period of latency.

Though the infection seems to be under control, during this latent phase, wave after wave of macrophages and other cells become infected with HIV. The immune system produces helper T cells, which mobilize killer T cells to fight the virus. This battle against HIV is continuous and ferocious. Yet the HIV-infected person feels perfectly healthy. There are no outward signs of infection, though HIV is present in blood and other body fluids. It is during this long symptomless stage that the virus is most often spread by people who are unaware that they have HIV.

HIV completely disrupts immune system function. In fact, it turns the immune system against itself. At some point during the long period of symptomless infection, HIV mutates in such a way that infected cells are able to pass the virus on to helper T cells in the lymph nodes. HIV kills the helper T cells it infects. Helper T cells are crucial to the immune system. Without helper T cells, B cells and killer T cells are not generated.

In the lymph nodes, HIV infects millions, then billions of helper T cells. The infected cells proliferate, each producing thousands of viruses, and then are killed. The lymph nodes become huge reservoirs of the virus. The lymph nodes become HIV factories where an unbelievable 100 billion new viruses are produced every day!

Viruses and Cancer

Scientists estimate that 10 to 20 percent of cancers involve viruses. The first connection was made by British physician Dennis Burkitt in 1961. While working in Africa, Burkitt noticed that a deadly childhood tumor occurred only in specific climactic conditions. Burkitt concluded that this cancer was caused by a virus carried by an insect native to this climate. In 1964, British virologist Anthony Epstein identified this cancer-causing virus, naming it Epstein-Barr virus (EBV). The cancer became known as Burkitt's lymphoma.

Since the discovery of EBV, five more cancer-inducing viruses have been found. Some forms of papilloma virus are linked to cancer of the cervix. Hepatitis B and C can cause liver cancer. Herpes virus 8, discovered in 1994, causes a skin cancer called Kaposi's sarcoma.

Besides his work in Africa, Dr. Burkitt was known for being one of the first doctors to recommend adding fiber to the diet to help prevent disease. He died in 1993.

Cancer arises through a multistep process, involving uncontrolled reproduction of cells. A virus that interferes with any step in the cell reproduction process might contribute to the onset of cancer. This may occur, for example, when viruses shut off cells' reproductive controls to get them to replicate viral genes or when viral proteins disable tumor suppressor genes.

The desperate immune system cranks out billions of new helper T cells daily. But they, too, quickly become infected with mutant HIV. The more helper T cells the body produces, the worse the infection becomes. Instead of fighting the infection, these desperately needed immune system cells are themselves infected, produce more HIV, and are then killed by it. The result is a relentless downward spiral in which the supply of helper T cells dwindles to near nothing and mutant HIV overruns the immune system.

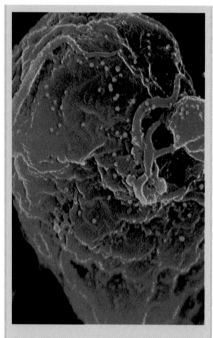

The small pink dots shown above are HIV budding off from the surface of an infected T cell. New antiretroviral medicines have had some success in disrupting the life cycle of HIV.

One microliter of a healthy person's blood contains about 1,200 helper T cells. A microliter of blood from a person whose immune system has finally lost its battle against HIV contains only 200 helper T cells. With so few helper T cells, the immune system is essentially destroyed. The infected person now has AIDS. During full-blown AIDS, up to 2 billion immune system cells are killed in the body every day.

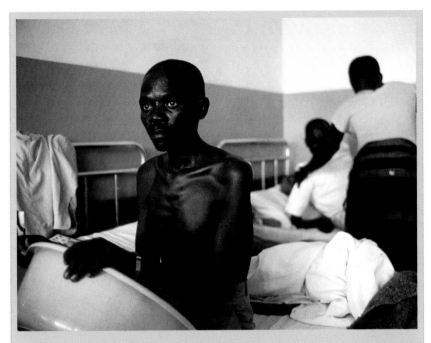

A man with terminal AIDS-related tuberculosis sits on his hospital bed in Gulu, northern Uganda. Lack of access to adequate health care and medicine, famines, cultural barriers, and social and political upheaval have led to an AIDS epidemic in Africa. The drugs to treat AIDS are also more expensive than most Africans can afford.

As the immune system is destroyed, the infected person becomes vulnerable to opportunistic infections—infections that a normal immune system could easily destroy but that overwhelm a body whose immune system is in ruins. Among the first opportunistic infections to arise is herpes virus 8, which causes a type of skin cancer called Kaposi's sarcoma. Other, often bizarre forms of viral, bacterial, and fungal infections attack the body. Wasting disease is particularly prevalent among African AIDS sufferers. Untreatable strains of tuberculosis or pneumonia are common. HIV itself infects the brain and

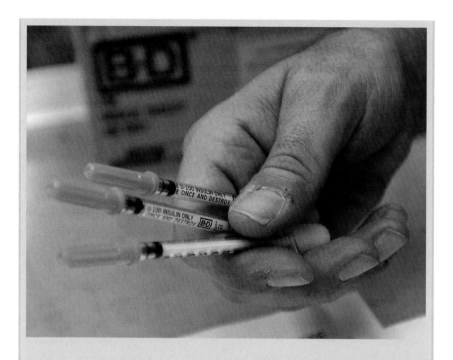

Sterile syringes like these are used in needle exchange programs, such as those in Boston, Massachusetts. Boston Public Health workers encourage intravenous drug users to exchange their used needles for sterile ones to prevent the spread of AIDS and other diseases.

may cause memory loss, tremors, epilepsy, and even psychosis. But AIDS also enables various herpes viruses, as well as bacteria that cause neurological diseases or tumors, to take hold and cause horrific brain diseases.

HIV is spread through body fluids, including blood, semen, vaginal secretions, and breast milk. All can contain both infected cells and infectious viruses. The current AIDS crisis is attributed to modern lifestyles. Intravenous drug users who share needles transmit HIV in blood. HIV is transmitted sexually. Many people today have multiple sexual partners, which greatly improves HIV's chances of spreading. In 2002, there were 5 million new HIV/AIDS cases, for a total of 42 million cases worldwide, including more than 3 million children under the age of fifteen. An estimated 28.5 million Africans are infected, with more than 2 million deaths in 2001. Worldwide, there are an estimated 14 million children orphaned by AIDS, 11 million of them in Africa. Nearly 500,000 Americans have died from AIDS. In the United States, there are currently more than 800,000 AIDS cases.

4 New Viruses and New Treatments

HIV was probably transmitted to humans from a similar virus that infected wild chimpanzees in Africa. This may have happened when people settled in a previously unspoiled chimpanzee habitat, loggers contracted the disease from contact with the chimps, or people ate infected chimp meat.

One of the main reasons for the emergence of new viruses is that people enter, occupy, and often destroy geographical regions that were previously uninhabited. Human invaders have no immunity against these new viruses, which are therefore devastating to their new hosts.

Rain forest destruction in particular has led to new viral infections. The infamous and lethal hemorrhagic viruses—Ebola and Marburg—emerged mainly from human intrusion into rain forests. Prior to human meddling, these viruses existed quietly and harmlessly among species adapted to harbor them. The Ebola virus first appeared in humans in a remote forested area of Zaire in 1976. It reappears periodically and has killed residents of Congo and gold miners in the rain forests of Gabon. Hemorrhagic viruses cause

Mad Cow Disease and the Meat Industry

In 1986, British cows became diseased. They staggered and trembled, then they died. Mad cow disease, or BSE (bovine spongiform encephalopathy), was quickly traced to the practice of feeding cattle the ground-up body parts from slaughtered cows. Turning vegetarian cows into cannibals by feeding them cheap dead-cow protein saved the meat industry lots of money in feed costs. But it also allowed BSE to spread wildly. By the late 1990s, millions of British cows and sheep were slaughtered to prevent the spread of BSE. By that time, several people had contracted and died from a human form of BSE, called Creutzfeldt-Jakob disease (CJD). Like BSE, CJD causes spongelike holes in the brain and is always fatal.

Evidence indicates that BSE and CJD are caused not by a virus but by an infectious protein called a prion. Prions are altered versions of a normal brain protein. The normal protein can be broken down and discarded by enzymes. But somehow prions change their form and

Infectious prions, like this one, may be the missing link between viruses and genes. Infectious prions cannot be killed by sterilization or antibiotics, making them more difficult to fight. There is no treatment for prion-caused diseases.

become "unbreakable." Enzymes can't remove them. Prions accumulate in the brain, where they continuously convert normal proteins into deadly prions. Prions also do not elicit an immune response in the body. Prion infection causes no inflammation, and it doesn't activate antibodies or killer T cells.

bleeding from all parts of the body. They are spread by physical contact, are highly infectious, and, in humans, are nearly always fatal.

The warming of the world's climate because of the combustion of fossil fuels (oil, gas, coal) is also spreading new viruses. When the West Nile virus reached New York from Africa in 1999, experts believed that the city's cold winters would kill the mosquitoes that transmit the virus. But the mosquitoes have survived several abnormally warm winters and have even spread farther north. Other insect-borne viruses, such as yellow fever and dengue fever, have also benefited from global warming. The insects that transmit these often-fatal viral diseases have increased their range as the climate has warmed. They are now able to live in regions that were once too cold for them.

These new viruses are not really new at all. They are old viruses adapted to nonhuman hosts in tropical climates. These viruses have "adopted" humans as hosts because of our intrusion into uninhabited areas and because of our altering of the world climate.

Vaccines and Treatments for Virus Infections

A vaccine is a virus preparation intended to be non-infectious to the human recipient but sufficiently potent to initiate an immune response. When

Dr. Jonas Salk, center, was responsible for the creation of a polio vaccine in 1952. Polio (poliomyelitis) is a viral illness that leads to paralysis by damaging nerves that control muscles. In severe cases, a person can lose the ability to move, may be unable to breathe without help, and may die. Thanks to Dr. Salk, polio is now rare in developed countries because most children are immunized against it.

injected into the body, the vaccine activates the immune system. In the course of fighting the limited infection, the immune system produces antibodies that stay in the body and safeguard against future infection.

There are several types of vaccines. Some noninfectious vaccines are made from dead viruses. The defunct viruses generate memory immune cells, but generally don't cause infection. Some polio vaccines are made this way. Another strategy is to make viruses out of pieces of viral proteins or even "naked" pieces of viral DNA. These vaccines activate the immune system to produce antibodies. Because they're incomplete parts of viruses, an infection cannot occur. This type of vaccine is being used successfully against hepatitis B. Attenuated or weakened viruses are grown in the tissues of nonhuman animals. When injected into humans as a vaccine, the weakened virus is unable to cause infection but does induce production of antibodies. Attenuated vaccines immunize against mumps, measles, and rubella (German measles). Attenuated vaccines have the advantage of producing lifelong immunity, something that noninfectious vaccines cannot promise. Finally, there are new vaccines whose DNA induces production of both memory B cells and killer T cells. The vaccine is made from DNA that codes for only a few viral proteins, so it cannot cause infection.

Sometimes vaccines are used to treat, not prevent, viral infection. Rabies vaccine is a case in point. Rabies reproduces slowly

Smallpox Vaccine

Smallpox is a horrible viral disease that used to kill millions of people. In 1796, Dr. Edward Jenner noticed that milkmaids who got cowpox blisters from milking cows never got smallpox. He concluded that the harmless cowpox blisters somehow made the milkmaids immune to smallpox. Jenner inoculated a young boy with cowpox taken from a blister on a milkmaid's hand. A few weeks later, he injected the boy with active smallpox. The boy did not contract smallpox; he had developed an immunity to it. Jenner had discovered and successfully used the first antiviral vaccine. By 1976, the World Health Organization's worldwide vaccination campaign eradicated smallpox completely.

in the body and usually takes a rather long time to reach its destination in the brain. A vaccine administered after infection usually gives the immune system enough time to mobilize and destroy the infection.

Aside from vaccines, antiviral drugs are designed to disrupt viruses during one particular stage of infection: during entry, uncoating, gene replication, or exit from a cell. To date, no drug can disrupt a virus's entry into a cell.

Military recruits like this one receive a wide variety of inoculations, depending on where they will be stationed and whether they might be exposed to biological weapons.

One new drug is able to disrupt the uncoating of the influenza A virus. The drug interferes with a viral protein that "unzips" the virus's coat, so viral genes cannot be released into the cell. Though this drug shows some promise, it cannot cope with influenza A's rapid mutation rate, which alters the targeted viral protein.

AZT, the drug used to treat AIDS, interferes with the replication of the retrovirus. Enzymes in the cell convert AZT into a protein that attaches to viral DNA,

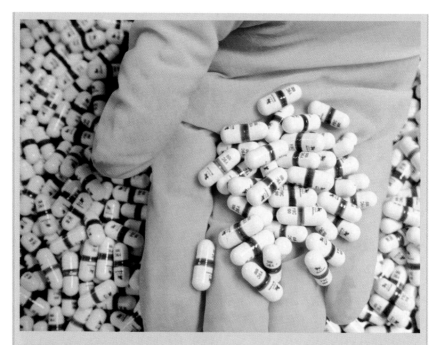

AZT, one of several drugs used to treat AIDS, acts by slowing the spread of HIV and fighting off infections, but it has side effects. AZT may cause a depletion of red or white blood cells, especially when taken in the later stages of the disease. If the loss of blood cells is severe, treatment with AZT must be stopped.

preventing the DNA from assembling. So replication of viral DNA is stopped.

In spite of new vaccines and new antiviral drugs, the rate at which viruses can mutate and adapt means that they will always be with us, in new forms both benign and deadly. But our immune systems also evolve. And since germs that kill off their hosts too rapidly and too efficiently doom themselves to extinction before they can spread, nature has a way of maintaining a balance between parasite and host, and there is hope for humanity.

Glossary

DNA (deoxyribonucleic acid) The hereditary material found in cells.

enzyme A protein that causes biochemical reactions to occur in cells.

gene A unit of heredity, made of chemicals (DNA) that carry the instructions for passing on traits from parents to offspring during reproduction.

host An organism that is invaded by and whose life functions support a virus or other parasite.

nucleus A membrane-covered part of a cell that contains DNA.

parasite A virus or an organism that lives on another organism and that gets food or protection from the host, which is often harmed.

protein A primary part of living things, containing substances consisting mainly of nitrogen and carbon—the "building blocks" of organisms.

receptor A part of the surface of a cell that is specialized for receiving a particular material, which attaches to the receptor.

RNA (ribonucleic acid) A substance found mainly in the cytoplasm that carries out DNA's instructions for making vital cell proteins.

For More Information

Centers for Disease Control
1600 Clifton Road
Atlanta, GA 30333
(404) 639-3311 or (800) 311-3435
Web site: http://www.cdc.gov

National Institutes of Health
9000 Rockville Pike
Bethesda, MD 20892
(301) 496-4000
e-mail: NIHinfo@od.nih.gov
Web site: http://www.nih.gov

Pan-American Health Organization
U.S. Headquarters
525 Twenty-third Street NW
Washington, DC 20037
(202) 974-3000
Web site: http://www.paho.org

The U.S. Department of Health and
    Human Services
200 Independence Avenue SW
Washington, DC 20201
(202) 619-0257 or (877) 696-6775
Web site: http://www.hhs.gov

World Health Organization (WHO)
Avenue Appia 20
1211 Geneva 27
Switzerland
e-mail: info@who.int
Web site: http://www.who.int/en

Web Sites

Due to the changing nature of Internet links, the Rosen Publishing Group, Inc., has developed an online list of Web sites related to the subject of this book. This site is updated regularly. Please use this link to access the list:

http://www.rosenlinks.com/germ/viru

For Further Reading

Facklam, Howard. *Viruses*. New York: Twenty-first Century Books, 1995.

Jussim, Daniel. *AIDS and HIV: Risky Business*. New York: Enslow Publishers, 1997.

Lemaster, Leslie Jean. *Bacteria and Viruses*. Chicago: Children's Press, 1999.

Monroe, Judy. *Influenza and Other Viruses* (Perspectives on Disease and Illness). New York: Lifematters Press, 2001.

Bibliography

Biddle, Wayne. *A Field Guide to Germs*. New York: Random House, 1995.

Crawford, Dorothy H. *The Invisible Enemy: A Natural History of Viruses*. Oxford, England: Oxford University Press, 2000.

Sompayrac, Lauren. *How Pathogenic Viruses Work*. London: Jones & Bartlett Publishers, 2002.

Index

About the Author

Natalie Goldstein has been a writer of science and educational materials for twelve years. She has written extensively about environmental, life, and physical sciences. Among her books are the *Earth Almanac, Rebuilding Prairies and Forests,* and *The Nature of the Atom.* She has worked for the Nature Conservancy, the Hudson River Foundation, the World Wildlife Fund, and the Audubon Society. A member of the National Association of Science Writers and the Society of Environmental Journalists, Ms. Goldstein holds master's degrees in environmental science and education.

Photo Credits

Cover © A. B. Dowsett/Photo Researchers, Inc.; pp. 1, 3, 4, 8, 10, 16, 19, 22, 25, 29, 34, 35 (background), 38, 41–48 courtesy of Public Health Image Library/Centers for Disease Control and Prevention; p. 6 © Don W. Fawcett/Photo Researchers, Inc.; p. 7 James King Holmes/Science Photo Library/Custom Medical Stock Photo; p. 9 © Stem Jems/Photo Researchers, Inc. pp. 11, 21 © Custom Medical Stock Photo; p. 12 © Mike Miller/Photo Researchers, Inc.; p. 13 © Alfred Pasieka/Photo Researchers, Inc.; p.15 © Biophoto Associates/Photo Researchers, Inc.; p. 17 © Science Photo Library/Photo Researchers, Inc.; p. 19 Hulton Archive/Getty Images; pp. 23 (left), 24 © Eye of Science/ Photo Researchers, Inc.; p. 23 (right) © Dr. Milton Reisch/ Corbis; p. 26 Custom Medical Stock Photo; p. 27 © NIBSC/ Photo Researchers, Inc.; p. 29 courtesy Albert and Mary Lasker Foundation; p. 30 © NIH, S. Camazine/Photo Researchers, Inc.; p. 31 © Malcolm Linton/Getty Images; p. 32 AP Photo/Chitose Suzuki; p. 35 (front) CNRI/SPL/Custom Medical Stock Photo; p. 37 AP Photo; p. 39 © Bob Krist/Corbis; p. 40 © Will & Deni McIntyre/Photo Researchers, Inc.

Designer: Thomas Forget; Editor: Jake Goldberg;
Photo Researcher: Sherri Liberman